Reading with Ricky
Rabbits, Builders, and Rainbows

Stories by Kathy Kranking
Illustrations by Christian Slade

. . . .

Contents

I Spy WITH MY LITTLE EYE

"I spy with my little eye . . . something red," said Ricky Raccoon. His friends Flora Skunk, Sammy Skunk, and Bizzie Beaver looked all around, each hoping to find the red thing before the others did.

Suddenly Sammy shouted, "There it is!" and he pointed to a little ladybug crawling on a leaf.

"That's right," said Ricky. "It's your turn now, Sammy."

The friends continued along the path in Deep Green Wood as Sammy tried to find something to stump his friends with.

"I love springtime," said Flora as the four friends walked along.

"Me, too," said Bizzie. "It's my favorite season."

As the group came up to Clear Creek, Sammy got a big smile on his face. "OK," he said. "I spy with my little eye something gray and hard."

The friends looked along the edge of the creek, where they saw dozens of rocks. Still more lined the bottom of the creek.

"Sammy, we know it's a rock," said Flora. "But there are tons of rocks. How could we ever pick the right one?"

"Try!" said Sammy with a grin.

The others sighed. Then Bizzie pointed to a smooth gray rock close to his foot. "This one?"

"Nope!" said Sammy gleefully.

FLORA WONDERS

Do you like to play "I Spy"?

Ricky pointed to a group of rocks just under the water. "One of these?"

"Nope!" Sammy replied as he giggled.

Flora laughed. "OK, Sammy, I guess you win this round!"

"Yay!" Sammy said. "I knew I would." He pointed at a tiny rock. "It was this one!" he said.

"My turn," said Bizzie. "I spy with my little eye . . . ," he said as he looked around the woods. Then he saw something unexpected. "I spy with my little eye an ear—wait a minute—two ears!" Bizzie said.

RICKY ASKS
....
Whose ears did Bizzie see?

"Ears?" Ricky asked.

"Yes! And now I see even more!" said Bizzie. He forgot about waiting for his friends to guess and headed toward a group of bushes. The others followed him, puzzled.

As they all peeked under the bushes, they gasped. Five little bunny babies were huddled together there.

"Wow!" said Sammy. "The ears belonged to baby bunnies!"

"They're so cute!" said Flora.

"But where's their mother?" asked Ricky, looking around. "The baby bunnies are all alone."

"I'm worried about them," said Bizzie. "They don't have anyone to take care of them. Maybe we should take them home with us."

"I can carry one of the bunnies in my pocket," said Sammy, pointing at his overalls.

Just then, Mrs. Cardinal came flying up and landed on a nearby branch. "Hi, everyone," she said. "What's going on?"

"Look, Mrs. C," said Flora. "We found some baby bunnies."

"Oh, what cute little babies!" said Mrs. C.

"We're going to take them home," said Sammy. "They need someone to take care of them."

"Oh, no," said Mrs. C. "The babies are fine. I'm sure their mother is around here somewhere. It's normal for mother rabbits to visit their babies only a few times a day, when they need to nurse. The rest of the time the mom stays away, so she doesn't lead enemies to the nest."

"Oh, that's a relief," said Ricky.

"The mother might even be watching from nearby, waiting for us to leave," Mrs. C added.

"Then I guess we'd better go," said Bizzie, and everyone agreed.

"Bye, baby bunnies," the four friends all said quietly.

"I'm glad those bunnies will be OK," said Ricky as the friends skipped down the path. "And now we can get back to our game." He pointed. "I spy with my little eye something over there."

BIZZIE WANTS TO KNOW

Do you think the baby bunnies will be OK?

"I know, I know," said Sammy. "Is it a tree?"

"Nope," said Ricky.

"Is it a butterfly?" asked Flora.

"No," Ricky said with a smile. "It's dinner, and it's at my house. Come on, everybody!"

Baby Rabbits

Look how quickly little bunnies grow.

1 Day Old

Bunnies don't have any hair when they are born. Their eyes are closed.

12 Days Old

In less than two weeks the bunnies have grown a full coat of fur, and their eyes are open.

30 Days Old

Bunnies are ready to live on their own when they are a month old. At this time, they hop away from their siblings.

The Very Best Home

Ricky Raccoon was feeling jumpy. He had been cooped up inside all morning.

"I think I'll walk over to Clear Lake and see what Bizzie Beaver is doing," he said to himself.

When Ricky got to Clear Lake, he saw Bizzie. The beaver was carrying a big stick in his mouth.

"Hi, Bizzie! What are you doing?" Ricky asked.

"Mm! Mm mm-mm mmmm," Bizzie answered.

"What?" Ricky asked.

Bizzie took the stick out of his mouth. "I'm adding sticks to my lodge," he said. "They help keep it strong."

Ricky followed Bizzie to the edge of the water. There, a big mound of sticks poked out of the water. It was Bizzie's lodge. To get in, Bizzie would swim underwater and climb up inside it.

"It must be fun to live in a lodge in the water," said Ricky. "I wish I could do that."

"You can use some of my sticks to build one if you want," said Bizzie. He pointed to a pile of sticks.

"Really?" asked Ricky. "Thanks!" He picked up two sticks. He looked at them. He looked at the water. Then he looked at Bizzie. "What do I do now?" he asked.

"Put some sticks in the muddy bank," explained Bizzie. "Then put more sticks on top. Fill in the gaps with mud."

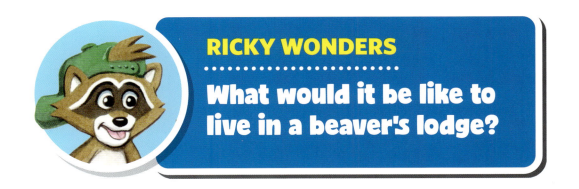

RICKY WONDERS

What would it be like to live in a beaver's lodge?

Ricky put the sticks into the bank. Then he added more sticks and a big scoop of mud. Ricky worked for a long time. Then he stepped back to admire his work. "What do you think, Bizzie?" asked Ricky.

Bizzie stopped working on his lodge and came to look. Ricky was muddy from head to toe. Poking out of the water was a messy pile of sticks. It was covered with gooey glops of mud.

"Uh, that's good, Ricky," Bizzie said, trying to be nice.

"Let's see how sturdy it is," Ricky said. He stepped onto the lodge. The sticks held for a minute. Then suddenly, the whole thing fell apart. "Yikes!" shouted Ricky. The next second, he was sitting in the water. The sticks from his broken lodge floated around him.

Bizzie rushed over to help Ricky out of the water. "Maybe you have to be a beaver to build a lodge," said Bizzie.

"Maybe you're right," said Ricky. He headed for home to get cleaned up. But on the way, he heard a happy song above his head. He looked up to see his friend Mrs. Cardinal sitting in her nest.

The bird's nest was made of twigs, dry grass, and vines. It was shaped like a cup. And it was very tidy compared to Bizzie's messy-looking lodge.

"Hello, Ricky," said Mrs. C. "What have you been doing today?"

Ricky sighed. "Well, I tried to build a beaver lodge. I wanted to live in the water like Bizzie. But I'm not a very good builder." Ricky looked at Mrs. C's nest. "It would be fun to live in a nest like yours— only bigger," he said. "Will you teach me to make one?"

FLORA WANTS TO KNOW

How is a bird's nest different from a beaver's lodge?

"Ricky, raccoons don't build nests. And they don't build lodges," said Mrs. C. "Some animals are good at finding a place to live without having to build it. You already live in the best home for you—your hollow tree."

Ricky waved good-bye and headed home to his house in the oak tree. When he got inside, he looked around.

"At least my house is cozy and dry," Ricky said to himself. "Not like a beaver's lodge. And I always have a roof when it rains. Not like a bird's nest," he added. Ricky thought for a minute. Then he smiled. "Mrs. C was right," he said. "I really do live in the best home for me!"

BIZZIE ASKS

Would you rather live in a bird's nest, a beaver's lodge, or your own home?

ANIMAL BUILDERS

Many animals build their nests.

A squirrel collects twigs, moss, and shredded bark. Then it uses them to make a nest in a tree.

A wasp mixes plants with spit to make a goo it uses to build. The goo turns into paper when it dries.

A weaverbird builds a hanging nest by weaving strips of grass together.

The Treasure Map

Ricky Raccoon was walking in Deep Green Wood when something caught his eye. A rolled-up piece of paper was poking out from under some leaves.

"What's that?" Ricky wondered. He picked up the paper and unrolled it. And as he did, his eyes got bigger and bigger. "Wow!" he said. "I've got to show this to the gang!"

A little while later, Flora Skunk, Mitzi Mink, and Bizzie Beaver were gathered around Ricky, looking at the paper he had found. It was a map of Deep Green Wood. A path was drawn through it and some X's were marked along the path.

"It looks like a treasure map!" said Flora.

"I wonder if a pirate dropped it," said Mitzi, giggling.

"X marks the spot, right?" Bizzie asked. "Do you think the X's show where there's treasure—like buried treasure?"

"I don't know," said Ricky. "Let's follow the map and find out!"

So the four friends got a shovel and headed to the first spot on the map: Clear Lake. Then Ricky read the clue that was near the X:

> *Sparkling brightly in the sun,*
> *This gem sure is a pretty one.*

"Hmmm, a sparkling gem," Bizzie said. "Maybe there's a diamond hidden here somewhere!"

FLORA WANTS TO KNOW

Have you ever gone on a treasure hunt?

The thought of finding a diamond got everyone very excited. So the gang began looking high and low. Ricky looked in bushes. Mitzi looked around the trees. And Bizzie looked under rocks and in hollow logs. Flora grabbed the shovel and began digging holes in the dirt.

Everyone was hoping to see the glint of a diamond as they searched. But after a long time of looking, they found nothing.

"Oh, well," said Ricky. He shaded his eyes from the sparkling lake. "Maybe someone already found the treasure," he said. "I bet we'll have better luck at the next spot. Let's go!"

So Ricky and his pals filled in all the holes they had dug and followed the map until they reached a pretty spot in the woods.

BIZZIE ASKS

What do you think happened to the treasure?

In the branches of the trees above them, bluebirds, cardinals, and other birds sang and hopped around. Ricky read the clue:

If you know where to look
You'll find these jewels:
Rubies, sapphires, and others, too.

"Wow, jewels . . . where do you think they are?" asked Mitzi. A bright blue jay and some goldfinches fluttered through the branches as the friends looked around for any sign of treasure.

"Do you think we should dig again?" asked Bizzie.

"We weren't able to find anything by digging before," said Flora.

"Let's go to Sunny Meadow," said Ricky, looking at the map. "That's where the next X is."

So Ricky and his friends headed to the meadow, where wildflowers bloomed in dazzling colors. Ricky read the clue from the map.

> *Here, a rainbow is the clue*
> *To treasure waiting just for you.*

They looked up at the sky.

"I don't see a rainbow," said Bizzie. "It hasn't even rained."

"And how could a rainbow be a clue to treasure?" asked Ricky. He frowned. "This map is useless," he said.

Everyone felt disappointed. "Well, at least it's really pretty here in the meadow," said Flora. "I mean, look at these flowers. Red, orange, yellow, purple—so many colors."

"Wait a minute!" Ricky said suddenly. "The clue said there was a rainbow. Maybe the flowers are the rainbow!"

Then the meaning of the clues dawned on Flora. "Come on!" Flora said, as she started running. The others followed her to the last spot they had visited.

"Remember the clue about the jewels?" Flora said. "Look at all these colorful birds! Bluebirds the color of sapphires. Cardinals the color of rubies!"

"Yes!" Bizzie said.

Everyone knew where to go next. The four friends ran back to Clear Lake. "The lake is shimmering in the sun!" Mitzi said. "It's the sparkling gem!"

"You know what?" said Ricky. "The map led us to many treasures. And they were right in front of us the whole time!"

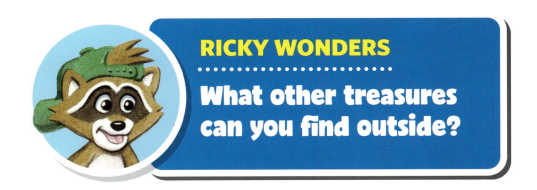

RICKY WONDERS

What other treasures can you find outside?

Flying Rainbows

ORANGE
Oriole

GREEN
Parakeet

RED
Cardinal

YELLOW
Tanager

Bird feathers come in all colors of the rainbow.

INDIGO
Indigo Bunting

BLUE
Blue Jay

VIOLET
Fairy Wren

31

Published by the National Wildlife Federation.

"Ricky and Pals" originally appeared in Ranger Rick Jr, a publication
for children ages 4–7 in the Ranger Rick family of magazines.

Kathy Kranking, Author
Christian Slade, Illustrator
Molly Woods, Reading Consultant

Photo and Illustration Credits:
Page 10: Jane Burton / Nature Picture Library (top), Sylvain Cordier / Nature Picture Library (bottom);
Page 11: Blickwinkel / Alamy Stock Photo (top), Richard Dorn / Alamy Stock Photo (bottom);
Page 20: Michael Quinton; Page 21: Jean-Louis Klein & Marie-Luce Hubert (left),
Mitsuhiko Imamori / Minden Pictures (right); Page 30: Roger Givens / DRK Photo (left),
Tom Vezo / Minden Pictures (top), Donald M. Jones / Minden Pictures (bottom);
Pages 30–31: Tui De Roy / Minden Pictures, Vecteezy (background); Page 31: Tom Vezo /
Minden Pictures (top), Donald M. Jones / Minden Pictures (left), Martin Willis (right).

Printed in the United States of America.

RangerRick.org

ISBN: 978-1-947254-27-5

Ricky and his friends team up to help children hone their reading skills—and make reading fun! Brought to you by the makers of RANGER RICK magazine, each book pairs fun outdoor stories with fascinating facts about animals. Collect all six!

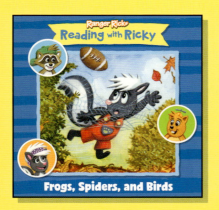

Frogs, Spiders, and Birds

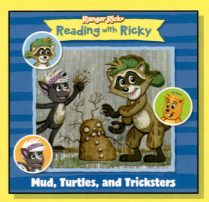

Mud, Turtles, and Tricksters

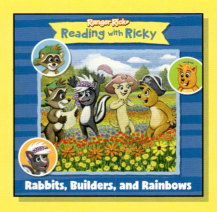

Rabbits, Builders, and Rainbows

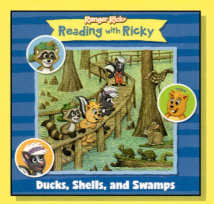

Ducks, Shells, and Swamps

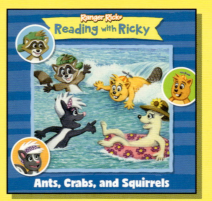

Ants, Crabs, and Squirrels

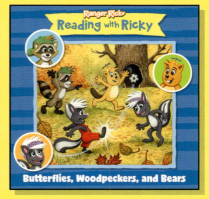

Butterflies, Woodpeckers, and Bears

The National Wildlife Federation believes that when we share our love of wildlife with kids, we can spark a lifelong passion to learn about, explore, and protect our natural world. The Federation's Ranger Rick family of magazines helps children of all ages discover and connect with nature so that they, too, become good stewards of the environment.